X CORANTO

Kit Ingram is an author of poetry and fiction. His illustrated novel-in-verse *Alice and Antius* was a *BookLife* Editor's Choice by *Publishers Weekly*. His work has appeared in *Ambit*, *Magma*, *Poetry Ireland Review*, and *The North*, and has been recognised by the National Poetry Competition, the Out-Spoken Prize, and the Bridport Prize. Originally from Canada, he now lives in London and runs Ingram Literary, a development studio supporting writers emerging later in life.

Also by Kit Ingram

Aqueous Red	(Broken Sleep Books, 2023)
Alice and Antius	(Penrose Press, 2022)
Paradise	(Ganymede Press, 2021)

CONTENTS

ISBN: 978-1-917617-14-7

The author has asserted their right to be identified as the author of this Work in accordance with the Copyright, Designs and Patents Act 1988

Cover designed by Aaron Kent

Edited and Typeset by Aaron Kent

Broken Sleep Books Ltd
PO BOX 102
Llandysul
SA44 9BG

X Coranto

Kit Ingram

Broken Sleep Books

There is no such thing as moral phenomena,
but only a moral interpretation of phenomena.

— Friedrich Nietzsche, *Beyond Good and Evil*

'What are the roots that clutch, what branches grow
Out of this stony rubbish?'

— T.S. Eliot, *The Waste Land*

AUTHOR'S NOTE

This work is a stitched map of detritus – lost headlines, collective stories, and personal confessions. It holds no allegiance to ideology but seeks the interstices where past and present, tragedy and triviality, collide. If you find the seams, pull them. If it unravels, let it. Every thread here longs to be unwound.

X, my new street, is flourishing
in crime –
the trees thumb-tacked with images
of MISSING power tools and teacup cats.
I try communing with the neighbours when I see them.
The lady next door told me
she's an actuary. Her livelihood is death.
In a veil of vapour,
she pointed to a slug on the vent cover
and said, *The tables know everything.*
This won't end well.

NOTICE
July 22, 1745

A husband reported his wife's necklace lost
or stolen ... seventy-two gold beads
with a locket. (I wonder what it held?
A twist of hair?
Sand from a seaside holiday?
How did the perpetrator, if applicable,
manage to trick it from her neck?
The closing line of the notice
reads: 'Half a guinea reward for an honest man.'
But much more, indeed, for a dishonest one.)

If I read an obituary,
I think: ego or privilege piping from the grave.
Who ends up on the page and who ends up lost
in the memories of family and friends,
assuming any?
The woman from 59 knocked on my door
and asked if I'd be attending Ed Trilby's funeral.
Who?
The man from 93, she said
and tapped on a block of serif font
in a newspaper clipping.
No mention of dying peacefully, she whispered.

NEWS
December 26 – 28, 1749

Late Sunday,
a woman genteelly dressed
was found dead along X,
near Old Kent Road. Allegedly,
on Saturday, she was seen trafficking
a bundle of linen.
(No name provided.
She was likely swindled
and discarded into the ditch.
That word 'genteelly' sounds like an overripe
apple fallen from a cart.)

CASUALTIES FOR THE YEAR 1749

Bit by a Mad Dog	1	Murdered	15
Broken Limbs	7	Overlaid*	32
Bruised	10	Poisoned	13
Choked with Fat	1	Scalded	2
Drowned	111	Self-Murder	48
Excessive Drinking	20	Smothered	11
Executed	26	Stabbed	11
Found dead	45	Starved	9
Frighted	3	Stifled	1
Killed by Falls and Accidents	42	Total	408

The genteelly-dressed woman is among these numbered. Where? She has hybrid potential, e.g. found dead *and* murdered. Her perpetrator could also have scared her to death. I'm no epidemiologist, but I'm most stricken by the suicides, a number only beaten by the victims of a murderous river running through the city.

*Overlaying is the accidental smothering
caused by a larger individual sleeping on an infant.

Nothing is safe from collection!
I asked, *What's in the cupboard under the stairs?*
You mean the spandrel, said Dr Molden,
pulling a jotter from the shelf. He flipped to the index.
Sixteen boxes of archival papers
beginning November '84 and ending whenever I—.
He dragged his thumbnail across his neck
as if beheading were the only way to stop him.

SALE BY AUCTION
January 9, 1769

Everything must go. The genuine
and entire household furniture,
China, and wearing apparel
of Mrs Stephens* deceased in her late
dwelling house on X.
Sale to begin at eleven in the morning.
(No end-time stated. Incidentally,
the doomsayer who now dwells in the dwelling house
shoots pamphlets through my letterbox.
They ask in Caslon font
WHAT MUST I DO TO BE SAVED?
Simple: be taken in by the doctor
or let the flames tickle you to ash.)

*Under common law, the property – and everything inside it,
including *her* – belonged to Mr Stephens, who presumably
submitted the ad and pocketed the proceeds.

The derelict industrial lot behind the house
is a hot spot for thieves and looters.
They cook over small fires, muttering gossip.
Last week, I climbed the garden wall
to glimpse their mafficking and saw
three foxes darting from my torchlight
into the cackling shadows.

NOTICE
May 5, 1771

The summer house Mr Lister erected
in his garden on X was greatly damaged
by some person or persons.
He calls for justice and will reward
anyone who shall, on his or her evidence,
convict the offender or offenders.
(Is there a precedent for convicting
non-human animals?
History says an outrageous punishment for failing
to meet a new definition of 'person'
is being skinned for a lampshade
or pocketknife case.)

Who can afford to live here anymore?
I manage on the beneficence of Dr Molden,
who pays the mortgage by writing
books on cross-dressing Victorians and other
better-known crimes.
Quid pro quo. I pay my rent by exhuming the dead:
bits of news lost in the archives.
One moment, I'm reading in his study;
the next, finding my life in the yellowing bodies
of news reports.

FOR SALE
January 20, 1790

X is offered for sale – twenty-nine
dwelling houses ('messuages') and gardens
each producing an annual rent
of fifty-two pounds three shillings.
(350 days' wages for a skilled tradesman, give or take.
X will be sold to a plummy man
in a silk waistcoat and frill at the neck.
Every year, he'll raise the rent
to fund increasingly exotic teas,
or perhaps tables inlaid with chess squares –
land plots in a growing empire.)

Today, BBC is a gobble of warnings:
Turkey Shortage at Christmas.
Stocks Culled Due to Avian Flu.
I asked Google for alternatives – 'flightless birds':
ostrich? Penguin?
Nothing on-continent!
I'd prefer to smuggle wine –
to get tipsy on white Burgundy
down in the cave where the *tsk* paddle hooks
glint in the blistering light.

CHRISTMAS CASUALTIES
December 1, 1790

A great mortality has broken out
among the turkeys in Norfolk.
Several of the dead bodies have been conveyed to London
for dissection, where it has been discovered
that the death of this delicious animal
has been entirely owing to a disease
which seizes them in the throat,
throws them into convulsions,
and deprives them of life in a few quick minutes.
(At Trinity, I roomed with a boy
who enjoyed oxygen deprivation
as a wind-up to climax.
I'd find him dangling from the closet rod,
meat in a butcher's window.)

The Victoria pub: shuttered.

Grocer: relocated outside the environs.

The butcher smiles in his bloodied apron,

but his days are numbered.

Harder to cut your own hair than your own beef,

so the barber is safe for now.

I queued with the rest for him

to cut my locks, approve and release me.

Car doors slammed in the distance, a racket of sirens.

I'd like a better version of this, I said,

pointing at my reflection. *Right, so the usual,* he replied,

cropping the sides to a shadow

and teasing the light with smiling blades.

I fell into the rhapsody of his breathing,

waking only when the door swung open –

his hands raised as if to give me a chance to flee.

COURT CIRCULAR
February 15, 1808

S. Varney, X Bermondsey.

Hairdresser to surrender on suspicion of murder,

February 17th at Guildhall.

(As a kid, I asked the barber why

the woman in the mirror was carrying her head.

He half turned, then looked back at my reflected eyes

and winced – like he'd remembered something.

Don't ask questions, he said, *unless you want to keep secrets.*)

INQUEST
October 28, 1825

An investigation took place
at Margate House on X, Bermondsey.
The body of an eight-month-old
boy was discovered,
smothered – a result of his mother lying upon him.
According to testimony, she awoke
to find her infant unmoving.
Mrs Parsons and her husband admitted
they were in the habit of going to bed 'a bit drunk.'
The jury returned the verdict of 'Accidental Death'
and condemned the negligence of the silent parents.
(Were they sober enough to grieve,
or did they toast their freedom with gin
in the glow of the new gas lighting?)

I lifted my window and saw a boy, about six,
peddling his bike and ice cream cone
into the thickening fog.
The woman from 93 followed
pushing a pram rattling full of green glass bottles.
Stop! Fuck's sake! Reggie!
His brakes screeched into an *Ah no!*
that popped into laughter.
I almost dropped it, he said, grinning,
but I caught it with my mouth.

WANT PLACES
July 22, 1829

A young man, aged about 30,
with a knowledge of tree pruning; ideally,
no objection to looking after a horse and chaise,
and making himself useful
in the kitchen.

CRAIGSLIST ADVERTISEMENT
post id: 6428917030

Seeking a male student, 18 – 29, for a live-in position.
Duties to include light cooking, gardening,
and organising various papers and collections.
Previous experience is advantageous, though not required.
Host will provide instruction.
Please apply with a CV and recent photo to Dr Molden.

I responded, not knowing it would land me
with a hoaxer and his rattle bag of tangled kinks.
Ever the scholar, he likes to refer to his excitations
by their Latin names:

Agalmatophilia – attraction to inanimate objects
Katoptronophilia – a fetish for mirrors
Claustrophilia – aroused by tight places

When I was younger
and coy as Rum Tum Tugger,
I'd visit the club and ask the man
with platinum hair and a gold incisor
if he had a little present for me. He'd pluck
a packet of white powder
from his jean's fifth pocket.
You can have it if you blow me. Your choice.

OXALIC ACID MISTAKEN FOR SALTS
April 14, 1834

An inquisition began when the body
of Mr John Bell of X, Bermondsey,
was found last Thursday.
Witness said, 'My God, Bell, what have you been taking?'
Deceased replied, 'Oh! I shall die: what have they given me?'
A local hairdresser was deposed, saying
he had known the deceased for 14 years
but was only guilty of giving him a bad shave,
and not whatever killed him.
A verdict was given of, 'Deceased, in consequence
of taking oxalic acid in mistake for Epsom salts.'
(Tragedy aside, I like this idea of the talking dead.
The dead dying again. Death *not* as an end
but as a question in search –
an itch in the spirit.)

If I have a kink, it's a fascination with history:
the secret, the bloody, the left-for-dead
in the shadows. What happened in these terraces
behind colourful shutters and doors?
Two centuries after this block was bricked
for the railway workers, the occupants have risen
from poorest semi-criminal* to broke
middle class. If you refinance
a mortgage of a million quid,
you get a landscaped garden, a kitchen conversion,
an under-floor cellar
to stave off decay and stiffen nipples.

EXTRAORDINARY DISCOVERY OF A MURDER
August 18, 1849

Yesterday, human remains were found beneath
the kitchen of a house near the Leather Market.
The man, identified as Patrick O'Connor,
was a wealthy gauger at the London Docks.
He had gone to the residence of Mr and Mrs Manning
for dinner but did not return.
The coroner determined the deceased had been shot
dead with two slugs embedded near his frontal bone.
On turning over the body, he saw the man's
false teeth dangling from his mouth.

*In his social maps of London, Charles Booth marked X as
populated by people who would do anything to survive.

I told Molden the 'Bermondsey Horror' story,
and he yawned so wide
I smelled the fish pie on his tongue.
I know it, he said. *The Mannings. Wife worked for a wealthy
family - had a taste for nice things.*
Money's always the motive. Railway shares, wasn't it?
A wee splash of that claret, will you?
You know, I said, *they described her as pleasant-looking*
like she couldn't possibly have shot a man
and slathered him in quicklime
to melt the evidence. Something about her dress, too.
Black satin with flounces.
A death gown! said Molden with a gap-toothed grin.

CHARLES DICKENS* TO *THE TIMES*
November 13, 1849

I was a witness of the execution at Horsemonger Lane
this morning ... When the sun rose brightly – as it did –
it gilded thousands ... of upturned faces, so inexpressibly
odious in their brutal mirth or callousness, that a man had
cause to feel ashamed of the shape he wore, and to shrink
from himself, as fashioned in the image of the Devil.
(Notably, the visages of the Mannings and their victim
appeared on collectable 'death cards'
with broadsheets detailing the murder. 2.5 million sold.)

*Dickens used Marie Manning as the basis for Mademoiselle
Hortense in the novel *Bleak House.*

If I'm feeling like a long black scream,
I imagine the doctor
slipping on a folio, limbs at off-angles, or
aspirating a bit of lamb confit
as I serenade him on the piano
with a gloomy nocturne.
I think of the authorities
sorting through his articles. Pieces *of* and *about* me:
nude photos, toenails,
ekphrastic scenes between
histories of academic twaddle.

A TERRIBLE CRIME
July 2, 1873

Early on Sunday morning at 31 X, loud screams . . .
He had a record of violence . . . chastising
his own son who escaped
with gashes at the neck. The culprit was caught
and with his injuries taken to hospital.
He dashed about the ward and corridors,
wrote in blood on the wall an appeal
and then leapt out the window.
Though in a precarious condition, he lingers –
a butcher, a professor of pain,
until trial.

The government can't say when
the pandemic will be over – maybe
never. We accept it
like the over-hot pillow we flip in the night,
like the frost in our hair
while we sleep in an armchair
in a loveless room,
like the ache in our tooth before we unscrew it.

RECURRENCE OF EPIDEMIC DISEASE
October 10, 1876

. . . London survived that violent outbreak,
but may be on the cusp of another.
Science seems unable to say *when* it arrives
whether it will be vicious, omnipresent.
We are bound to ask whether
the conditions pre-empting this scourge are here again.
Some say that many deaths are caused
by the destroying angel*;
others by the frenzy official warnings create.

On the 11th of October, the daughter, 8, of an A&E nurse
died after one week with the disease
and one night of convulsions.

*Mushroom tip: See a white stalk and gills and run for the hills!

The voice teacher at 41 X passed by with a baby
girl. I saw her face like a glistening
pearl between waves of fleece.
So peaceful, I said.
She doesn't sleep, sighed the woman,
but she can match the pitch of the smoke alarm
or that bit in The Magic Flute
when the Queen sings about hell's vengeance
boiling in her heart.
Her name, I asked?
Oh, Emily.

INFANTICIDE
September 28, 1883

The wife of a piano maker dwelling on X was charged
with the drowning of Emily Burton, her infant child,
also with attempting to drown herself
in The Docklands east of London Bridge.
Following the inquest, a guilty verdict was given,
with the mother-turned-murderer
removed to Clerkenwell House of Detention*.
(Why the botched suicide? A lack of ambition?
A loosened corset? A sudden rush of God?)

*The site was later redeveloped, and parts
of the prison's underground vaults remain
beneath the Mount Pleasant Mail Centre today.
Many claim the site was – and *is* –
haunted by a singing spectre.

True crime gripped the Victorians.
The cortisol hit from reading about Jack the Ripper
was safer than picturing their own
deaths on the streets –
say, on the conduit to the market
or behind the factory where the lights don't reach.
Safer than freeing their inner violence, too.
Murder was sentenced to the page – became
entertainment. And the righteous ate it up
like good little deviants.

I want to be taken to the police station!
If you do not take me, I shall murder someone tonight!
I am Jack the Ripper.

—William Griffiths, a young drunk man on the street (1888)

If you don't have me, you don't know what happened.
You're going to think about me, but it's not going to be me,
because you have no proof. This city is mine.

—Marek Hecko, a young man-turned-murderer (2023)

In the front garden of 41 X,
a father consoled his daughter,
who said Mrs B embarrassed her in front of the class,
made her repeat the secret
she'd whispered to Melanie, her friend.
What was the secret? he asked,
but instead of an answer, I heard the fat
spatter of rain on the window.

DISGRACED HEADMISTRESS
October 24, 1899

Mrs Baddeley,
headmistress of the infant department
at X Board School was charged
with assaulting Alice Carter, a child of seven years.
On the day in question,
Mrs Baddeley was trying to give a singing lesson
when Alice interrupted with a sudden jig.
In her usual punishment,
the mistress bid the child repeat her moves
in front of the class.
When she refused, the mistress coaxed her
with sweets. When that too failed,
she broke a cane over Alice's backside.
Until then, Mrs Baddeley claims
she always treated the children
with the greatest kindness.

A reek in the house like an earthworm-y muzzle.
Outside, the planters vomit
mud onto the garden stones, and foxes track through,
leaving prints that diffuse
in the rain, unrelenting
since Saturday. I've placed saucepans
under all the leaks
except in the conservatory
where Molden is sorting through bills
unalarmed by the scuttering mice.
I'm enlightened by the search engine, which confirms
rodents, driven to survive,
take to higher ground during flood events
while humans pray for divine intervention.

FLOODING IN SOUTH LONDON
October 17, 1903

2000 houses were flooded with sewage,
damaging many goods and livelihoods.
The Mayor of Southwark, addressing
the Council, said the runaway
water was a major risk to the health of inhabitants ...
Fever hospitals flooded, boilers extinguished,
patients carried out in the night amidst streams of rats.
The Local Government Board says more must be done
to prevent this from happening again.

A spigot of postal workers
clogs the end of my street.
The easiest way through is to smile,
thumbs-up, honk the horn –
not pause to chat about the collapse
of capitalism, or its gaudy late stages.
I got lost between tongues,
polishing worst-case scenarios.
Did anyone hear me in that dirge of despair?
Are my letters locked in a red van
abandoned at the depot?
Waylaid by bureaucrats, stolen and redacted –
like the morning post-bender?

CHRISTMAS POSTAL STRIKE THREATENED
December 6, 1911

While most of the 70,000 postal servants
favour a strike during the Christmas rush,
Union leaders hesitate.
Workers demand greater agitation
among the top brass. Their grievances:
unpaid overtime, soaring costs,
unmitigated suffering, death.
(Perhaps it's time to draft a timetable
for afterlife socials, a pub
with a banging quiz.)

Afternoon broke like a thief through the blinds,
spilling over the doctor, naked,
in his armchair, stroking
a cat with oracular eyes, half-closed.
I suspect he didn't know he was about to die,
Molden said. *Or he would've run.*
Maybe the stray wanted to be found, I said.
Like this? He held up the feline's crushed skull.
The weight of all these, he muttered,
pointing to the apocalypse of toppled books
and Billy doll boxes blocking the only way
out of the house.

SOLDIER'S PONY
March 22, 1919

Robert Donoghue of X was summoned
for working his pony to the brink of death.
He claimed he was troubled, 'gassed' in France,
and needed the pony to make a living for his family.
A veterinary surgeon said
the animal was past working age
and should be promptly retired.
The defendant was fined forty-two schillings.
(Roughly six days' wages for a skilled tradesman –
just enough to eat for two weeks
or starve a little slower.)

Horatio, my frenemy from a few doors down,
with too much time and too many selfies,
sent me a photo: wingback chair,
a pint of ice cream
nearly covering his genitals.
Choose between these ice cream flavours, he wrote,
devil-emoji grinning.

1. Chocolate / Vanilla / Strawberry / **Cherry**
2. Green tea / **Irish cream** / Banana / Blueberry
3. Mint / Oreo / Pecan / **Chocolate chip**
4. Orange / **Caramel** / Jelly bean / Peanut butter
5. Pineapple / **Pistachio** / Grape / Lemon
6. **Raspberry** / Mango / Bubblegum / Cotton candy

Your fetish is exhibitionism, he texted
with a link to an Austrian neurologist.

ICE CREAM FACTORY ACCIDENT
July 22, 1938

The inquest of the body of Spencer Riley of 25 X
determined the cause of death as internal decapitation.
The coroner said it was Mr Riley's job to remove cups of ice cream
off the conveyor belt from a filling machine.
When the ice cream filler jammed, pressure built up,
and the cylinder burst in his face,
severing the ligaments that joined his skull to his spine.

Ticker tape tragedies pass through me.
What do I feel?
I hear others through the walls,
scratching to get out.
When was the last time my throat hurt
from laughter?
If I feel anything, it's like milk unravelling
in the blackest tea.

PROBLEM OF SEX OFFENDERS
March 11, 1949

According to a new report,
'Punishment without treatment is not
likely to have a beneficial effect. Indeed,
it can make these offenders worse and thus more likely
to repeat their offences. In a high proportion of these cases
imprisonment without treatment may have consequences
to the community more dangerous
than to the offenders themselves.'
(This concern for the safety
of 'offender' and 'community' – haunting abstractions –
reads like dictation from a brain on ice.
Where is the evidence that treatment
works? Where is the proof that abusers lose their cravings
after mandated therapy?
Where are the high-quality differential studies
showing that a monster has changed under its gilded mask?)

Sunday: Molden said grace before dinner.
With his eyes full of candlelight,
he thanked God, instead of me, for making
a cassoulet from a recipe
penned by his perished wife.
I thought of adding a paste of cherry pits to his –
a bit of *ha ha* for me.

HOMOSEXUAL INQUIRY URGED
December 5, 1953

The Home Secretary has been requested
by the Church of England Moral Welfare Council
to launch a comprehensive investigation
into the issue of homosexuality.
The council's executive committee
suggests that the inquiry cover the implications
of new psychological research on the determination of guilt,
the imposition of punishment, and the impact of the prison
system on a homosexual inmate.
(Naturally, the church has a vested interest –
its sanctuaries lure mollies, masochists,
closet cases and rapists.
Abuse reports now number in the hundreds,
but the true toll, over centuries,
is buried under tongues.)

I gave a spiel on the history of patronage.
Without it, no Caravaggio
painting shadows around the light of brutality.
His eyes: full stops that saw the end of art's fakery.
The doctor wheezed and asked me
if art is what I've been doing
at my computer screen full of nudes
instead of news.
I told him if he gives me a fiver,
I'll buy him a tub of cherry ice cream
and let him watch me
eat it.

FREED OF SEX CHARGES
March 17, 1968

A man who had pleaded guilty
to gross indecency
and buggery with a boy
had his conviction overturned
with the changes to the Sexual Offences Act.
(No word on whether this benefits the boy.
Perhaps he'd be happier without
his aggressor knocking on his door years later,
telling him how little he's changed.)

The man from British Gas
interrupted my revisions to say
Your power bills are unusually low for a household of two.
While he fiddled with the meter,
I noticed the bride from the wedding cake
glaring at me,
so I broke off her head.
My whole body hung, suspended in a question:
Is this what it costs to be free?

MINISTER CONDEMNS POWER BILLS
February 11, 1972

The Minister for Industry told the Commons
he condemned inflating energy costs –
that frightening people into installing meters was criminal.
'The Electricity Council,' he said, 'were swindlers –
frauds bullying the public for profit.'
'Just this year,' he continued,
'an elderly woman, unable to pay her bill, killed herself.'
'Shame! Shame!'
he cried to a silenced house.
(Imagine the uproar if he spoke the whole truth:
One suicide is a tragedy;
thousands of elderly freezing to death
in their homes,
talking only to ghosts,
is a scandal to be papered over.)

I opened the shutters to the smell of woodsmoke –
an old morning in Bermondsey,
when the tanneries woke
on streets tracing back to the Domesday book.
Wood was always cheaper
than burning fossils for fuel.
Little has changed.
Survival costs ratchet up with no quick release.
Molden says the best way to stay warm
is to dance for him – a swish of hips,
a black satin dress.
The last time, I say.

TWELVE FACE CALL BOY CHARGES
November 19, 1984

28 men were questioned by police
as part of investigations into an alleged call boy ring*.
Of those, 16 were arrested and released on bond.
The men are accused of committing serious sexual offences,
including 'indecent assault on young boys.'
(What qualifies as a 'non-serious' sexual offence?
Who decides?
The men freed with stacks of bills,
or the boys ripped from their price tags,
damaged goods?)

*Some definitions of call boy:
1) A male sex worker who accepts appointments by phone.
2) A boy or young man who summons actors when they're due on stage.

Midsummer's Day and war at its prime.
The actuary next door said,
The enemy is lying about the death count.
Thousands were dead from indiscriminate shelling.
She clacked her veneers.
The fascists are propagandists, not accountants.
She asked if I'd heard about the dozen men
excavating a surprise in the garden of number 33.
It happens more than you think, she said.
Are we talking about a body? I asked.
No, though there could've been if they hadn't—
she spun an invisible globe slash cartoon bomb,
and snipped the air
as if to sever a sparking fuse.

BOMB DEFUSED
June 24, 1993

The block of terraces on X
was temporarily evacuated last night
as disposal experts defused a World War II bomb
after thirty hours of labour.
(They say the best way to disarm a dictator
is to drill into their heart
and dissolve
the sinister crystals at the core.)

'Missing' is a chilling word. But so
is 'found'.

GONE, PRESUMED FORGOTTEN
June 3, 2005

In Britain, over 200,000 people go missing each year.
Could you visualise any of them?
The typical image is of a junkie
calling out from filthy blankets.
Not so for the Piano Man*,
the most notorious missing person in memory.
Seven weeks ago,
this mute and mystifying young man
was found wandering near the water –
soaking wet, the labels ripped from his cashmere suit.
His plight has attracted global attention,
yet his identity remains a mystery.
(Some claim he's a Parisian busker,
a Swedish mystic, a Canadian eccentric,
a Czech pianist. Others call him a lost soul, a wanderer.
Why has no one claimed his name?
What kind of silence erases a face like his?)

*He's allegedly blessed with a musical touch,
treating hospital staff to performances of
everything from 'Chopsticks' to Chopin.

Molden knows our game is running out of play.
Where will I go? The hollows creak like ghosts.
An utter depression of soul, he murmurs between us.
I moved every box to the attic,
letting light foam through the windows, spill
over grids of our sedimented skin.
In a reverie-turned-mission, I carved
notches in the crossbeams with a power saw I nicked.
Some days, I think the only way to survive is to kill
the dark things revving in our ears.

HAUNTED HOUSE SEEKS FRIENDLY OWNER
March 9, 2019

The vice president of the London-based
Society for Psychical Research claims
the majority of hauntings can be explained
though 20 per cent cannot,
'which does make you wonder,' he says,
'if in some way, these things are generated by the people
they're around. All we know is we cannot ignore them.'
(Is a ghost free to leave?
Or are they the property of the homeowner
till death does them part?
I asked Horatio how to get rid of the doctor.
There's only one way, he said, *and it will hurt
until it doesn't. What happens then?* I asked,
but he slipped into a wisp of agarwood incense.)

Most nights, I dream I'm drenched, dripping.
I climb down with my saw from the attic
into a room full of ruin.
A raven waits atop a rubble of ice cream tubs
and porno magazines.
Its grey irises catch flashes of lightning,
like a scene from a gothic poem.
I know the raven is another doctor in disguise.
I need him to hold still, but he beats his wings and flies
into a splintering crack in my chest.

MAN DISCOVERED DEAD
UNDER PILES OF CLUTTER
April 17, 2020

While obeying the lockdown order,
a Canadian man was crushed to death
when his bedroom ceiling collapsed.
Under the debris, the search team found evidence
that damaged crossbeams in the attic
had snapped under the load of hundreds of boxes.
Officers waded through
an immense collection of sexual paraphernalia,
textbooks, sheet music, and historical newspapers –
so blackened by spores, they dissolved at a touch.
Neighbours reported seeing the owner
leave the property earlier that evening.
He could not be found for comment.

ACKNOWLEDGEMENTS

I couldn't have written this book without the invaluable resources of The London Library. *X Coranto* took shape in its magnificent reading room, alive with the echoes of history. I'm deeply grateful to the patient staff who guided me – pointing me to the right buttons to click and shelves to explore.

A special thank-you to Karina Lickorish Quinn, author and senior lecturer in creative writing at Royal Holloway, University of London, for her enthusiastic support and insightful feedback during the early stages of *X Coranto*. Sometimes, a little nudge is all we need to silence our inner critic.

I am immensely grateful to those who took the time to read and endorse this book: Andre Bagoo, Troy Cabida, John McCullough, Kirsten Norrie, and Karina Lickorish Quinn. Your inspiring work and generous support mean the world to me. To early readers, Ruth Rosengarten and Károly Tendl – your enthusiasm kept me going.

Finally, heartfelt thanks to Aaron Kent and the team at Broken Sleep Books for believing in *X Coranto* and for their commitment to championing diverse voices and the stories that need to be told.

LAY OUT YOUR UNREST